F P.L.

WORLD OF ROBOTS

BY ELIZABETH NOLL

da Vinci Si

MEDICAL ROBOTS

BLASTOFF! DISCOVERY

Bellwether Media • Minneapolis, MN

Blastoff! Discovery launches a new mission: reading to learn. Filled with facts and features, each book offers you an exciting new world to explore!

This edition first published in 2018 by Bellwether Media, Inc.

No part of this publication may be reproduced in whole or in part without written permission of the publisher.
For information regarding permission, write to Bellwether Media, Inc., Attention: Permissions Department,
5357 Penn Avenue South, Minneapolis, MN 55419.

Library of Congress Cataloging-in-Publication Data

Names: Noll, Elizabeth, author.
Title: Medical Robots / by Elizabeth Noll.
Description: Minneapolis, MN : Bellwether Media, Inc., [2018]
   | Series: Blastoff! Discovery. World of Robots | Audience:
   Ages 7-13. | Includes bibliographical references and index.
Identifiers: LCCN 2016055087 (print)
   | LCCN 2017004539 (ebook) | ISBN
   9781626176898 (hardcover : alk. paper) | ISBN
   9781681034195 (ebook) | ISBN 9781618912923
   (paperback : alk. paper)
Subjects: LCSH: Robotics in medicine–Juvenile literature.
   | Robots–Juvenile literature. | Medical technology–Juvenile
   literature. | Medical innovations–Juvenile literature.
Classification: LCC R857.R63 N65 2018 (print) |
   LCC R857.R63 (ebook) | DDC 610.285/63–dc23
LC record available at https://lccn.loc.gov/2016055087

Editor: Christina Leaf   Designer: Jon Eppard

Printed in the United States of America, North Mankato, MN.

TABLE OF CONTENTS

MEDICAL ROBOT AT WORK!

Geena slumped in her chair. She didn't want to learn about her dad's surgery. The hospital was boring. The surgeon talked super fast and used a lot of words she did not know. Geena heard the word "robot." Then the surgeon led them into the operating room.

There was a chunky plastic desk with a viewfinder in the top half. A machine with four arms stood next to a hospital bed. At the end of each arm were shiny metal instruments.

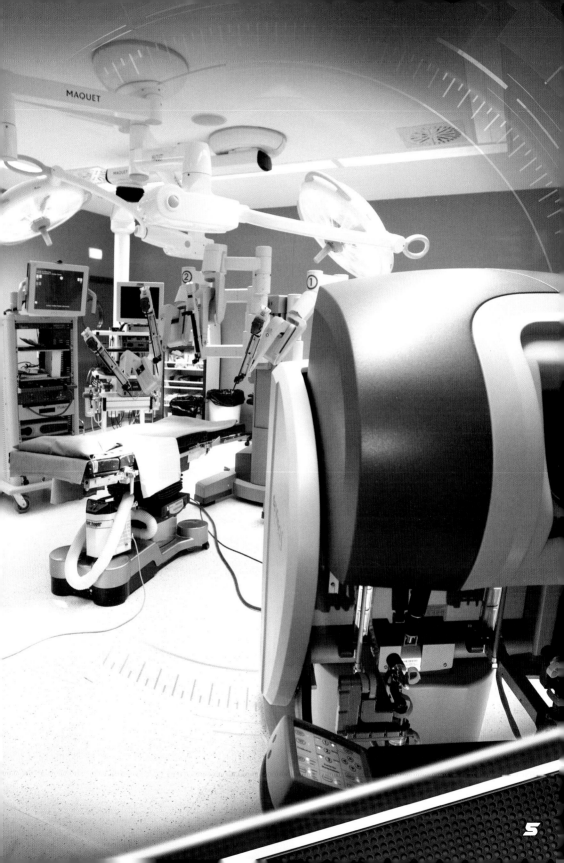

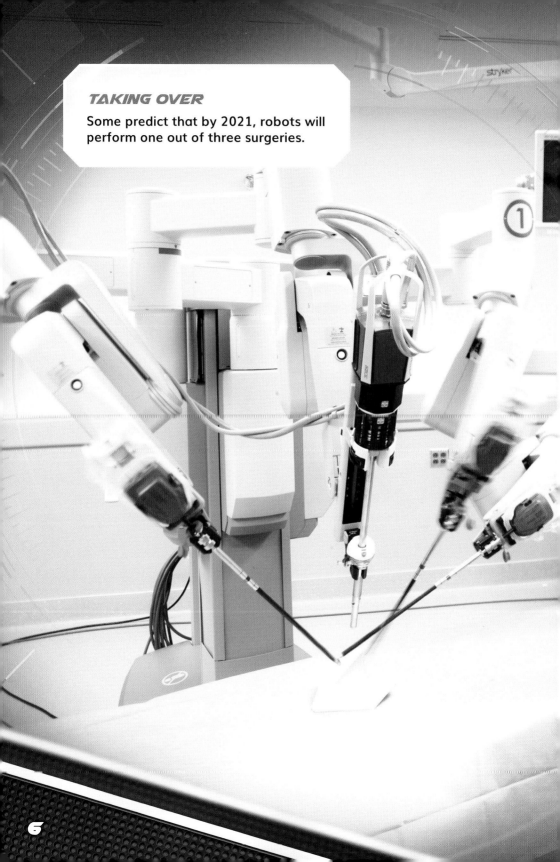

TAKING OVER

Some predict that by 2021, robots will perform one out of three surgeries.

The surgeon sat at the desk. When he moved the controls, the machine's arms rotated. The tiny pinchers at the ends of the arms picked up a piece of paper on the bed. Two pinchers worked together to fold the paper into an airplane.

The surgeon explained that the robot would operate on Geena's dad while he ran the controls. The robot's tiny, **precise** cuts would heal quickly, he said.

For the first time ever, Geena wished their hospital visit could last longer.

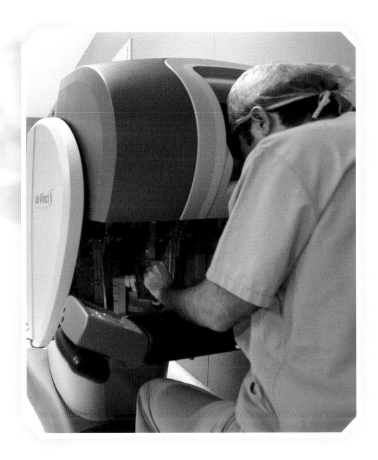

WHAT ARE MEDICAL ROBOTS?

Medical robots help doctors and patients in many ways. Their movements are precise and steady. Some can lift heavy things. Robots can also do boring jobs without making mistakes.

Surgical robots help by making surgery less **invasive**. This means less pain for the patient. **Therapy** robots can help injured people learn to walk again. Robots can help nurses by lifting people out of beds and into wheelchairs. Other robots help package medications and get them ready for patients.

ROBEAR

Ekso
exoskeleton

The most common kind of medical robot is the surgical robot.

In order to operate, a surgeon must be able to see inside the patient. Also, there must be room for their hands to move. Without robots, this means making a large **incision**. That takes a long time to heal.

Surgical robots can perform **laparoscopic surgery**. They make several small cuts instead of one big one. A tiny camera goes inside the patient so the surgeon can see. Patients with smaller incisions heal faster. They also have less pain.

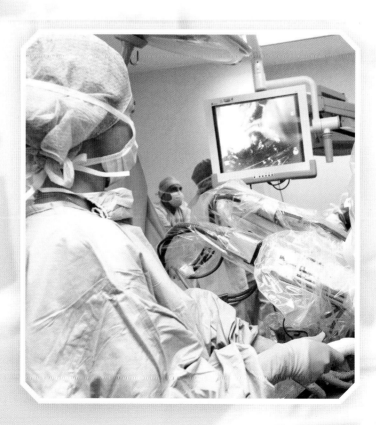

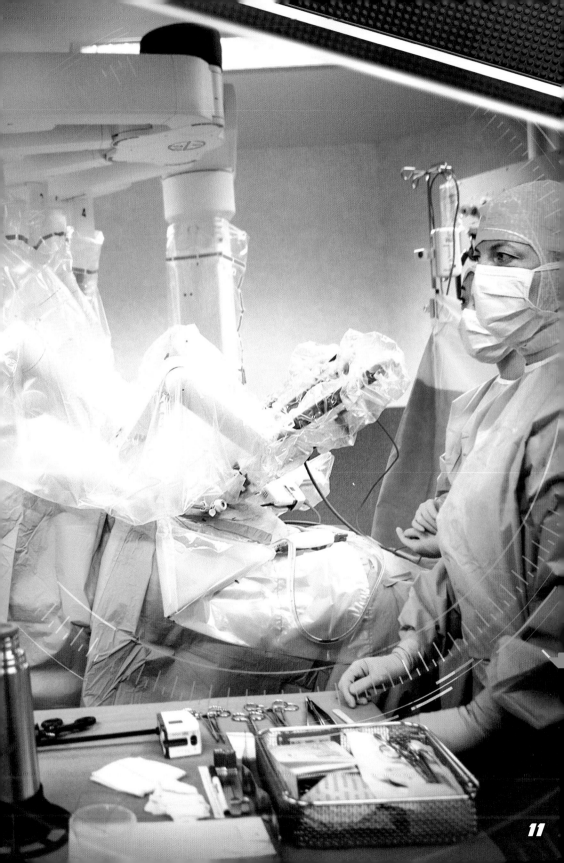

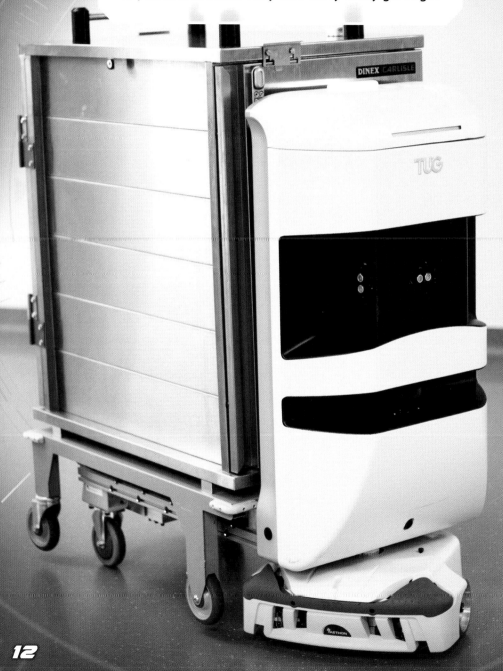

HOSPITAL HELPERS

Robots called TUGs are used at more than 140 hospitals in the United States. TUGs move on their own. They bring medicine, food, and other things to patients or staff. They also carry away garbage.

Many new medical robots comfort patients and help them relax. MEDi is a small robot that talks to kids who are nervous at the doctor. Keepon Pro helps children with **autism**. For them, the little yellow robot can be easier to talk to than adults.

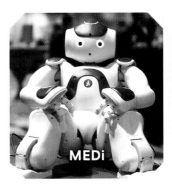
MEDi

Some robots, called **exoskeletons**, help people who are **paralyzed** walk. They can also help injured people relearn how to walk. One, called ReWalk, straps on over the legs and has motors at the hip and knee.

ReWalk exoskeleton

Pharmacists get medicine ready for patients. They find the right pills and count out the correct amount. Then they give the pills the proper label. If a patient gets the wrong medicine or amount, it could be a fatal error.

Some medical robots can count pills or package medicine for prescriptions. They are extremely careful and fast. Unlike humans, they never get bored or lose track.

THE DEVELOPMENT OF MEDICAL ROBOTS

Medical robots have only been around for about 30 years. A surgical robot came first. In 1985, the PUMA 560 helped with difficult surgeries and brain **biopsies**. Scientists then invented other surgical robots, including the PROBOT and the ROBODOC.

NASA also began to research robotic surgery for astronauts in space. They worked on methods for telesurgery, or ways surgeons could operate from far away. Other groups thought this technology could help wounded soldiers on battlefields. The research led to the ZEUS and da Vinci robotic surgical systems. In 2000, the government approved the da Vinci system for laparoscopic surgery.

SMOOTH OPERATORS

Surgeons have used the da Vinci robot for more than three million operations.

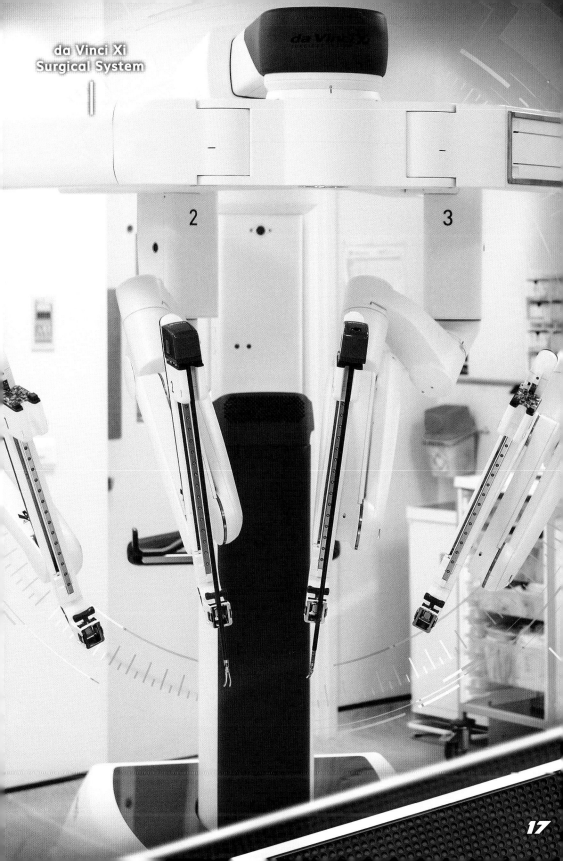

da Vinci Xi
Surgical System

illustration of a nanobot
attacking cancer cells

Since da Vinci, medical robots have become more common and varied. Some, like robotic exoskeletons, are very new. Others are still in the lab, like cancer-fighting **nanobots**.

As technology and robot parts become cheaper, more people can afford to build robots and experiment with them. For instance, robots have tools called **sensors** to figure out their surroundings. Sensors are like our eyes and ears. As sensors become cheaper, robots become cheaper. This means more people can try to come up with new ways to use robots in the medical field!

SaeboFlex exoskeleton

MEDICAL ROBOT PROFILE:
DA VINCI

Da Vinci is a human-controlled robot used to perform surgeries. Robotic arms work on the patient. Across the room, the surgeon sits at a console and moves hand controls that direct the robotic arms. Using the da Vinci system guarantees that the "hands" performing the surgery will always be steady.

A camera and light are attached to one of da Vinci's arms. This lets the surgeon see inside the patient and accurately direct da Vinci's movements.

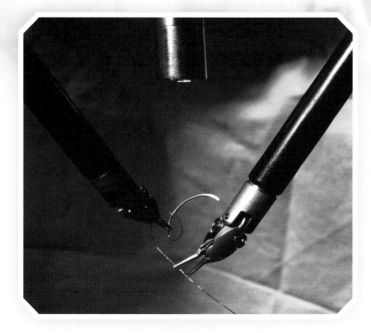

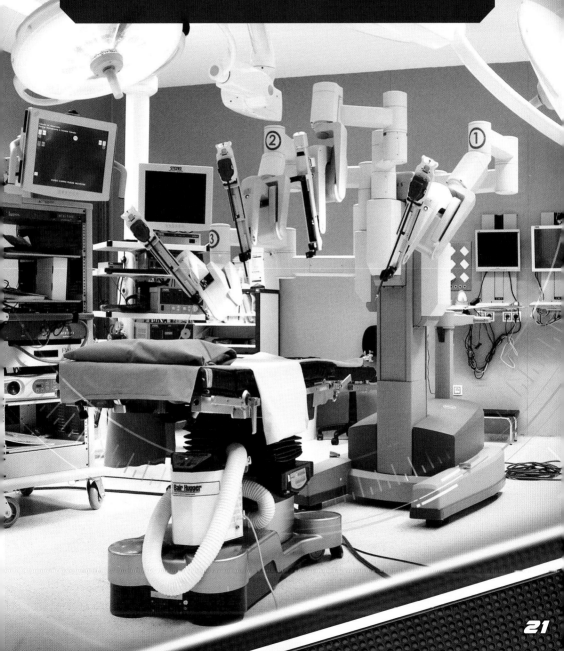

Name:	da Vinci
Developer:	Intuitive Surgical, Inc.
Release Date:	1999
Function:	performs minimally invasive surgery
Parts:	command console for surgeon, plus patient-side cart with robotic arms

MEDICAL ROBOT PROFILE:
RIBA

RIBA is the first robot to be able to lift and move patients. Scientists created it to help nurses. Nurses lift patients from beds to wheelchairs and back again many times a day. This often causes back injuries. Help from RIBA could prevent this.

RIBA has a friendly, bearlike face with big, round eyes. Its arms are strong and made of a comfortable, soft rubber. There are more than 200 sensors in each arm. These tell how to safely move patients.

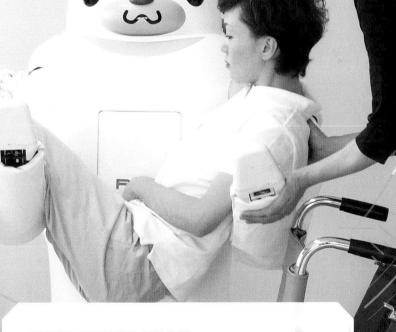

Name:	Robot for Interactive Body Assistance
Nickname:	RIBA
Developer:	RIKEN-TRI, Japan
Release Date:	2009
Function:	nursing care
Size:	4.6 feet (1.4 meters) tall; weighs 397 pounds (180 kilograms)
Load:	can lift 134 pounds (61 kilograms)

NEXT GENERATION

In 2011, RIKEN released RIBA II. The new version can lift heavier patients and has a larger range of motion. Scientists are still working on another updated RIBA, named ROBEAR.

MEDICAL ROBOT PROFILE:
RIVA

RIVA is a strange-looking robot. It looks like a tollbooth or a walk-in freezer with windows. Inside the shiny metal walls, RIVA combines medication that goes into **syringes** or **IV bags**. Then it labels each by medication or patient name. RIVA is fully **automated**. Nobody is directing its movements with a remote control.

In most hospitals, pharmacists combine the medication for IVs by hand. RIVA's makers say their robot's work is safer and faster than a human's.

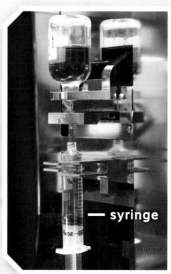

— syringe   IV bag —

Name:	Robotic IV Automation
Nickname:	RIVA
Developer:	ARxIUM Inc. (formerly Intelligent Hospital Systems Inc.)
Release Date:	2008
Function:	combining medication for IV bags and syringes
Size:	8 feet (2.4 meters) tall; 5 feet (1.5 meters) wide; 10 feet (3 meters) long
Speed:	combines up to 60 doses per hour

MONEY MAKER

RIVA costs about $1 million. Many hospitals make that back in just a few years since they have fewer errors that waste medicine.

MEDICAL ROBOT PROFILE:
ROBOT-RX

ROBOT-Rx is like a huge vending machine with a metal arm that moves around very fast. The arm grabs a package of medicine from a storage rack. It takes the medicine to a different area and drops it into a bin or patient-specific envelope.

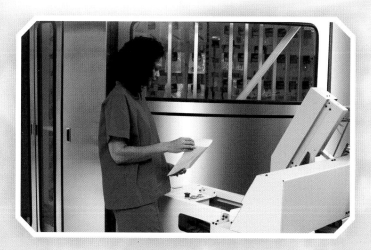

ROBOT-Rx uses bar codes to find the right medicines and the correct patient. These codes also help it handle returns and restocking. With ROBOT-Rx doing **repetitive** tasks, pharmacists have more time to help patients.

Name:	ROBOT-Rx
Developer:	Automated Healthcare, currently owned by Omnicell
Release Date:	1992
Functions:	filling and restocking prescription medication
Size:	variable
Speed:	counts 6,000 to 7,000 doses per day

THE FUTURE OF MEDICAL ROBOTS

Experts predict that we will soon see many more medical robots. Some will be doing everyday tasks like counting pills, taking blood, and carrying food. A space robot might be performing surgeries on astronauts without direction from a doctor on Earth. Others may be inside humans! Robots the size of a red blood cell may be fighting cancer or monitoring our health.

Other medical robots will almost certainly be saving lives in ways we can only imagine right now.

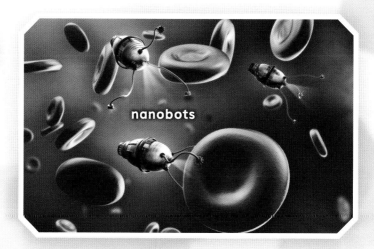
nanobots

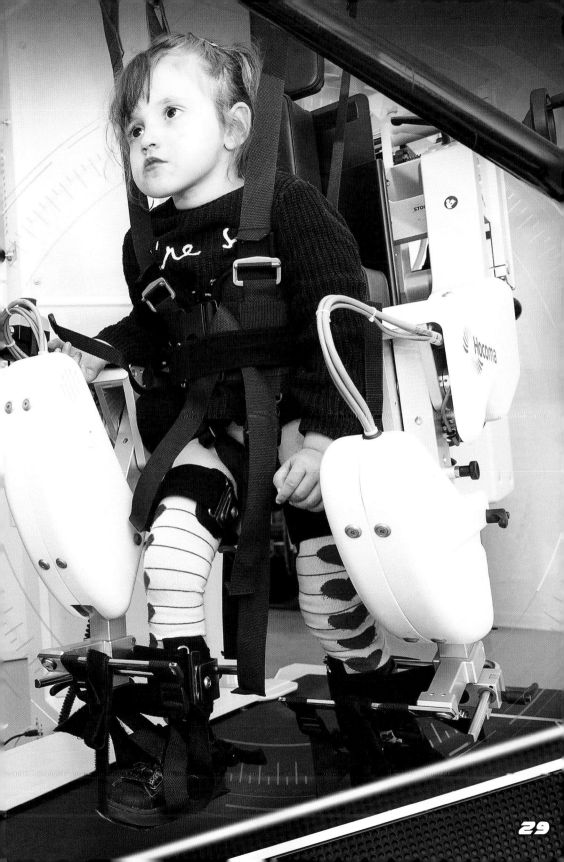

GLOSSARY

autism—a disorder that affects how people communicate and socialize

automated—able to run without human help

biopsies—procedures in which tissue or cells are cut from a human body to check for disease

exoskeletons—shells or other hard structures on the outside of the body

fatal—deadly

incision—a cut made during surgery

invasive—something going where it does not belong

IV bags—bags that hold liquid medication that goes into patients' veins through a needle; IV stands for intravenous, or going into the veins.

laparoscopic surgery—minimally invasive surgery that uses a video camera and thin tools to make small incisions

nanobots—tiny robots that are about the size of a red blood cell

NASA—National Aeronautics and Space Administration; NASA is a U.S. government agency responsible for space travel and exploration.

paralyzed—unable to move parts or all of the body

pharmacists—people who prepare medicine from doctors' prescriptions

precise—exact

prescriptions—written directions from doctors for the preparation and use of medications

repetitive—something that is repeated

sensors—devices that respond to light, pressure, sound, or other physical changes

syringes—devices with needles that inject fluids into the body

therapy—the treatment of a disorder or injury of the body or mind

TO LEARN MORE

AT THE LIBRARY

Faust, Daniel R. *Medical Robots*. New York, N.Y.: PowerKids Press, 2016.

Mooney, Carla. *Wearable Robots*. Chicago, Ill.: Norwood House Press, 2017.

Swanson, Jennifer. *National Geographic Kids Everything Robotics: All the Robotic Photos, Facts, and Fun!* Washington, D.C.: National Geographic, 2016.

ON THE WEB

Learning more about medical robots is as easy as 1, 2, 3.

1. Go to www.factsurfer.com.

2. Enter "medical robots" into the search box.

3. Click the "Surf" button and you will see a list of related web sites.

With factsurfer.com, finding more information is just a click away.

INDEX